Praise for
Greetings from Bullhead Couontry

"Yes, there are fish here: bullhead, carp, and the rarely caught, sometimes mythic northern pike. Vetsch, an expert scavenger himself, with a sharp eye for telling detail and an acute ear for the way people really talk, has assembled a remarkable body of poems cast as youthful memories in Minnesota. The focus is largely on family—his mom, dad, grandma, grandpa, uncle, and others. He digs deep into relationships, family dynamics and roles, acknowledging foibles, sugarcoating nothing (this is not Lake Wobegon). His extraordinarily deep sensitivity to the difficulties and sometimes harsh realities of people's lives is sad, poignant, and very funny all at once. Greetings from Bullhead Country is a delightful, wondrous, affecting book that will stick with me."

—Mark Gustafson, author of *Sowing Seeds: The Minnesota Renaissance & Robert Bly, 1958-1980*

"I met Scott Vetsch in a dive-bar in Northeast Minneapolis. He was onstage telling us about fishing for carp and bullheads and hanging with his pals and telling hilarious tales about his family of colorful characters. Greetings From Bullhead Country is a collection of bruised and scruffy tales with poor boy truths, always just this side of lawless."

—Fizz Kizer, Singer/songwriter

"Scott Vetsch's Bullhead country is a place where life is lived in color and with all five senses and then some. People there are 'bullheaded' in the way of stubbornly claiming the reality of their lives against America's class oppression and prejudice. Scott grew up among scrappy, resilient people who knew that we keep alive the truth of who we are and where we come from through our stories."

—Thomas R. Smith, author of *Medicine Year* and *Storm Island*

"Scott is funny. Funny in that stealthy understated way where the humor sneaks up on you. A poem will start with a seemingly harmless, purposely prosaic title, a situation unfolds in the verse, and then bang, the last line suddenly throws a floodlight back onto the title and it all comes into focus. Poets, of course, do this all the time. Scott is good at it, by turns eliciting a burst of laughter, an ironic twist, a poignant wistfulness, or a sad realization. Yes, there are serious poems too, where Scott sees in his upbringing a background of circumstances that led to a pre-determined set of choices, habits and limitations. We all deal with this, and gradually pick up perspectives, knowledge and tools that might help us accurately see what we've been dealt, accept it and glory in the things at hand — while not forgetting to laugh."

—Phil Heywood, Guitarist

"Reading Welcome to Bullhead Country is like walking through a series of small streams. The water is cool or even cold, the current in the streams is gentle or a little stronger, and it is fun. But all the streams flow into a river. Once you read through this book you smile and then chuckle and then laugh out loud. But read the poems and stories again and they all flow together and then you are in the big river where you discover the water is deeper and the current is stronger than you first thought and then, you are carried away. Read this once and then read it again."

—Jim Stowell, Storyteller

Greetings from
Bullhead Country

CALUMET EDITIONS
Minneapolis

FIRST EDITION DECEMBER 2025
Greetings from Bulhead Country
Copyright © 2025 by Scott Edward Vetsch. All rights reserved.

No part of this book may be used or reproduced in any manner whatsoever without written permission except in the case of brief quotations used in critical articles and reviews. For information, write to Calumet Editions, 6800 France Ave. S., Suite 370, Minneapolis, MN 55435

10 9 8 7 6 5 4 3 2 1
ISBN: 978-1-962834-64-3

Cover and interior design by Gary Lindberg

Greetings from Bullhead Country

POEMS

Scott Vetsch

Minneapolis

Dedicated to Mom and Dad

Table of Contents

Family Dynamics 1
Bullhead Country 7
Our Neck of the Woods 11
Hazel and the Holy Rollers 13
Nepotism 17
1915 19
Back When Grownups Told the Truth 21
He Turns the Channel Without Saying Hi 25
Social Studies 27
Lenny Just Stared 29
Buckethead 33
Religious Teachings 37
Epiphany 41
Sorties 43
Grandpa's Living Will 45
Seventeen 49
Spike and the Rubber Vomit 51
Easy Money 53
Dad's First Psychedelic Experience 55
My Mother's Stint as Outlaw 59
The Isanti Bounty Boondoggle 67
International Affair 69
Lester 71
Florence Told 75
Grandpa's Birth Control 77

Ruins	75
New In-Laws	81
Who Took the "K" out of Fun-Pac	83
Dad's Quest for Perpetual Motion	85
Motherhood Before the Microwave	87
After the Storm	89
Tornado Alley	91
Choosing Darkness	95
Bottom Feeder's Blues	97
Ice Fisher	99
Delroy Calhoun Said	101
A Son's Inheritance	103
Good Intentions	105
The Fisherman's Wife	107
The Weight	109
Pissant Hill	111
Lost Currency	115
Frieda Sums it Up	117
It Used to be All Woods Up There	119
Carl and the Beanstalks	121
Best Corn I Ever Ate	123
The Intellectual	125
Proletarian Writing Workshop	127
Meditations on the Old Man	129
About the Author	139

Also by Scott Vetsch

Tilt-A-Whirl

Family Dynamics

Dad always tried to get Mom to do his work;
"Men's work".
Mom's job was cooking, accounting,
child-rearing, keeping house.
Dad was breadwinner,
plus household maintenance.

Like Tom Sawyer,
he tricked Mom with ploys of family fun
and togetherness.
Enlisted by fate of gender,
it served my purposes
to wheedle with him,
attempt to fill the ranks of our misery.
My sister, busy cutting the heads
off her Barbie dolls,
looked up anxiously from her play.
If Mom gave in, she too would be drafted.

Mom would help if her labor
could shorten my weekend's
indentured status,
let me run off with my friends sooner,
her own flesh and blood.
Her motive was not lost on Dad,
he emphasized how many hands
lighten the load.

One weekend he talked Mom
into splitting firewood.
She swung her axe and
that straight-grained red oak
split with a single whack.

Dad noticed she liked the
feeling of accomplishment and
conjured the myth of
"Goliath Oak-The Forest King."
Mom stood before that bandy-legged bastard,
axe replacing slingshot, taking him down with every
stick she split.
Dad spun the tree's character
like an effigy of himself,
a carnival barker drawing out
Mom's resentment,

positioning the target,
allowing her to strike back.

A pile of split wood grew around Mom's feet
as Dad set the next piece on the block,
each blow another grudge riven.

It was so positive,
so empowering and that was something
Dad couldn't stand for long,
and like teasing cats,
even at the risk of losing his
new-found splitting mechanism,
like the Luddite he was
he couldn't resist
throwing in a twisty chunk of elm.
Mom's axe sank and stalled.
Say what you want about Dad,
in the end he favored truth.

Another time he set Mom to
pulling rusty spikes from
recycled oak beams.
Dad's challenge was to keep Mom going,
keep her believing it was fun.
But the oak worked against him.

Nails driven before WWI did not easily
give up their seating,
and the old wood handled claw hammer
Dad gave her
quickly cracked.

This didn't work as well as the
splitting had and worriedly Dad
handed her another hammer.
Mom's impatient levering cracked it too.
Dad fetched a crate of hammers
from the shop and
gave her another.

Mom quickly understood her only
chance for escape.

Like a machine-gunner
manning the last foxhole defense
against an invading horde,
she could only abandon her post
when she ran out of ammunition.
Dad should have shifted strategies and
given her a crowbar,
but kept handing her hammers.

"See!?" she wailed,
ankle deep in a rubble of broken handles
and impotent heads.

"See!? I can't do this, I'm just a woman."

Bullhead Country

It's all there were in those
muddy creeks and sloughs,
besides carp, suckers, and
a few hammer-handle northerns.

A worm-baited hook cast out on
braided black line,
red and white bobber pulled under,
slippery whiskered fish with stinging barbs,
yanked from the water and
flung to shore wriggling
at the end of a cane-pole.

My little sister and Billy,
too young to fish by themselves,
were set one in front of the other
in the grass on Grandma's Point,

gripping a cane-pole between them.
When the cork went under,
they hoisted that bullhead like a pole-vaulter
out of the water and over their heads.

To clean bullheads
Dad drove a sixteen penny spike
through the top of their heads and
nailed 'em to a post.

Immobilized,
he could gut 'em without getting stuck
by their mucous-covered spines to
strip off their slimy skin
with a pair of pliers.

I got good at sliding my hand up the tail,
thumb and middle finger
behind those needle-like pectoral spikes,
web of my thumb snugged behind the dorsal,
gripping them to remove the stubborn hooks.

Before eating bullhead I asked grandpa
what it tasted like.
"Muddy." he said,
inscrutable as his reply to the

taste of snapping turtle:
"Like chicken."

An old Bulgarian couple lived next door.
They kept a small orchard
and a large garden.
We had a path behind their house,
ran through daily,
our fishing poles sticking straight out.

They said they'd take any fish we didn't want.
We made them our reason to fish and
after daily buckets of bullheads they said
please no more.

In bullhead country you don't swim
without a pair of old sneakers on your feet.
Bullheads wriggle into the muddy bottom,
dorsal spine straight up.
Stepping on that made a
foot-full of green sand-burrs
no big deal.

Fishing in the Mill Pond, I yelled
"Dad, I got one and it ain't no bullhead."

I hoped it was a northern,
like the one on the Schmidt beer sign
jumping out of the water,
expensive lure hooked in its bony jaw.
The Land of Sky Blue Waters,
that mythical place
I desperately wanted to live.

There were northerns in the creek,
it was a possibility.
The fish surfaced and it was green.

"Dad I think it's a northern!"
He ran down where I fished under the bridge,
where it flopped in the sand.

It was a carp.

It didn't put me on that beer sign.
It wasn't a story for Field and Stream.
But I felt good,
it wasn't a bullhead.

Our Neck of the Woods

Grandma said a Real Man
walked outside to spit
but a True Gentleman
removed the dishes
from the sink
before he peed
in it.

Hazel and the Holy Rollers

Grandma came from a freethinking background. Her mother was a Quaker. Her father, a divine do-it-yourselfer, entertained the Methodist minister when he turned up Sunday afternoons to play checkers and discuss life.

She'd outlived her contemporaries. The black diphtheria, accidents, whiskey, and war, had taken the best, left her with the kids she hated in school; the tattletales and the goody two-shoes.

Widowed and in her nineties, she was the last human alive on the farm.

Grandma wasn't much for TV. Living alone out there, she drank coffee and read cartons of trashy romance novels that she and her friend Lucille passed back and forth. They'd known each other since school, both witty and irreverent. Lucille had a bum hip and didn't get out much, unless one of her sons drove.

Grandma loved conversation. She sat up til four in the morning with visitors. Started out with coffee and ended up with brandy. Only now her late-night philosophizing cohort had thinned down to me or dad.

Grandma was a make-do kind of person. If you didn't have strawberries you used rhubarb. If you couldn't travel you read The National Inquirer. If you didn't have visitors you made-do with evangelists.

The farm was between Zimmerman and Crown on County Road 4, a main stem for short-cutting truckers, salesmen, evangelists and bar-hopping drunks. Grandma had no patience for salesmen or drunks. She found missionaries weak-minded, but admired their moxie to get out there. When they came to her door she invited them to pull up chairs at her kitchen table. There were Mormons, Seventh Day Adventists and Jehovah's Witnesses. Grandma lumped them all together as Holy Rollers.

You could say Grandma had an interesting spiritual life. She passed herself off as Methodist, but an hour into that conversation and you realized she played her dogmas fast and loose. She loved Native American beliefs, wasn't adverse to a little UFO speculation, and then there was that unearthly chanting, heard from behind her bedroom door when she finally went to bed, that sounded like a wrestling match with some dark deity.

Grandma wanted me to say I believed in Jesus even if I didn't. If you stated this oath you were granted eternal life. She didn't see a problem with an all-knowing god knowing whether you really meant it or not. I told her when I died I'd look for her out there and that seemed to satisfy her, a kind of dogpaddle through the protoplasm, a wading through eternity, floating in that great expanse like the survivors of some maritime disaster, calling out for loved ones, gripping on to the wreckage.

Grandma believed spirituality was an open-ended question but those Holy Rollers started shifting in their chairs at this kind of talk. They were trained to push a doctrine but Grandma pushed back. Fear and shame had no effect on her. She only sought a good-natured exploration of the unknown.

After hours of philosophical end-runs, the Holy Rollers were on the defensive, just trying to get out. They left Grandma each week with a few more pamphlets to read and Grandma left them with a renewed challenge. They hadn't come to question their own beliefs, but Grandma loved a good debate. The Holy Rollers could save three souls on a good day, but Grandma took their entire afternoon and left them with nothing.

Nepotism

Back when Dad was lookin'
for a 55 gallon drum
to tune his outboard in,
it sure was handy
having Aunt Irene
shacked up
with Max Gorney
the Junkman.

1915

Grandpa told about shining northerns
on Elk Lake during the spawn.

They hauled the boat out after dark.
In the stern Uncle Fritz
poled the shoreline while
Grandpa knelt in the bow,
gripping lantern and spear.

Next morning they sold 'em by the pound
behind Cal Olsen's Meat Market.

One night he noticed
what looked like a log
submerged in the shallows
and scratched it with a tine
of his spear.

A mammoth pike
slashed its tail
into deep water,
boat sloshing
in the wake.

"You get one chance,"
Grandpa said,
"You gotta mean business."

Back When Grownups Told the Truth

One Saturday Dad and Grandpa took me fishing on Lake George. Rickety, paint peeling, beer-joint cabins ringed the shore like thirsty mutts. We followed a boat rental sign down a path between banished washing machines, engine blocks, and 55 gallon drums. At a picnic table overlooking a wooden dock, rental business was conducted to the twang of Ernest Tubb, as the vast dishpan of Lake George lapped its Anoka Sandplain shore.

My head was filled with the mythic northern pike flashing on the Schmidt beer sign as vivid blue damselflies helicoptered above lotus green lily pads. A parrot on a perch said things Grandpa laughed at.

While Dad decided between 14 feet and 16 feet, between a five horse Johnson and a six horse

Evinrude, the rental man's Salem smoking wife
thought I might enjoy seeing their two pet squirrel
monkeys. She led me into the living room where
they perched like crabby little men atop a curtain rod.
Monkeys don't crap in a box like cats so the curtains
were stained and the house smelled like a diaper pail.
She picked up one monkey and carried it outside to
the table where the grownups drank beer. A black
kitten jumped up and the monkey pulled it around
by the tail, rear feet dangling. The kitten, starved for
attention, didn't care.

The rental guy cracked another beer and said there
was a northern in the lake that had broken the lines
and dreams of every fisherman that hooked it. Lures
and hooks dangled from its snout like stolen jewels.
On still summer nights you could hear them rattle
like broken chains when it shook its head. It was man
against fish.

We trolled the weed-line in the dog-day heat, sun
beating our hatless heads, dragging daredevils and
sucker minnows round and round through that
swampy bathwater without a strike. Hour after hour
we held our poles and hoped. That jade Johnson five-
horse chugging hypnotically, yellow ball of the sun
sinking into the trees. Feverish, I wondered if you

could hear the lure's rattle as it swam, or if it raised its head above the surface and shook them like a Loch Ness Monster. In the twilight, Dad cut the engine and grandpa tied us up to the dock, fish-less except for our bucket of half-dead minnows.

The rental guy was sorry we'd struck out, said you can't win 'em all and showed me a couple boards in the dock he had to replace. Said one night, lying in bed he woke up to a heckuva racket. It was a clear moonlit night and he looked out the window in time to see that damned fish smash through his dock and rattle those hooks at him for no reason but pure mean. He said the necklace of spoons and crankbaits hanging from that ugly mug had to be worth thirty bucks.

On the way home I asked Grandpa how a fish held itself out of the water to shake its head like that, how it could breathe when it did, not tear its skin on all that splintered wood, and how could it eat with a mouthful of hooks. Grandpa said it sounded like one helluva fish, probably part crocodile and asked if I ever heard about the time it rained so hard he nearly drowned.

He Turns the Channel Without Saying Hi

In my childhood house,
when Dad came home
from work,
sister hid under the bed,
and Woody Woodpecker
"Guess who'd" from the tube.

I could've hid
but sat on the couch,
even as the Ford's engine
died in the driveway.
Could've run but waited,
winced at his steps on the gravel,
stared motionless
as the screen door opened.

Scott Vetsch

I feared that song at five P.M.,
that smart-assed blue bird
who cackled at bigness,
then pecked without mercy
the head of some lunk in a suit.

Before dinner in many homes,
neighborhood kids laughed
like crying in their hearts.

Realization of the Mummy

My favorite Halloween costume
was a toilet paper Mummy,
wrapped tightly round
a white union suit,
ends fluttering like in the movies.

Marching in the Halloween Parade,
ego held in only by my windings,
I could walk right up to people
I knew and remain unrecognized,
edge into a group and
gesture with voiceless familiarity.

I was feeling pretty omnipotent til
some kid asked how I went to
the bathroom.

Social Studies

In third grade we watched a film
concerning family life in Japan.

I remember a boy eating his school lunch;
sticky-rice balled around pieces of fish.

Later under the monkey bars
I imagined Uncle Ben's soaked
in salty butter,
squeezed around a chunk of hotdog.

Lenny Just Stared

Our ninth-grade gym teacher
was a Vietnam Vet.
On the last day of the archery section,
he dressed up in camouflage,
painted his face
and hid out in the woods,
instructing the class to find him.

We stalked in
loose packs,
blue gym-trunks,
sweatshirts, and
skinny legs,
through alder
and dogwood,
until group by group,
we came

upon him;
standing rigid as
a fencepost.

We milled around
like puppy dogs,
arrows strung,
bows at ready,
embarrassed,
wondering what
we were supposed to do
when we found him.

Buckethead

I don't trust anyone who gets
too gimmicky, too gadgety,
when it comes to escaping labor.
My Dad would spend an afternoon
perfecting a block and tackle,
rather than muscle
what needed muscling,
would patch a rag of a shirt
before spending a quarter
at Goodwill,
would rail against a plastic gas can
when the only thing that forced him to buy it
was his own temperament.

When I was a kid he tried
to keep me busy at home,

keep me out of trouble
after school.
I should've got a job,
not waited for him
to find me another box to paint
or more holes in the driveway
to fill up using earth scraped
from the gopher mounds
that burst from our yard
like acne.

When Dad bought a sandblaster
I became the instrument
that transformed rusty metal
into smooth painted implements.
He built a blasting room
in the corner of the garage,
installed a barn-fan to suck
the silica from the air.
I wore a dusty Airforce parka
and welding mask,
dark lenses replaced by
the rectangles Dad cut
from old window glass.

He cut stacks cuz the sand
etched them so quickly

and as visibility decreased
so did productivity.

Mom objected to the long hours
Dad prescribed in the sanding booth
to make a man of me,
worried about the dangers
of inhaled silica.

Dad soothed her concerns by
designing original safety gear.
He found a five-gallon tin bucket,
turned it upside down and
cut-out a rectangular window.
He then hinged a sash
which could be swung open
or fastened shut
like a deep-sea diver's helmet.
He drilled a hole in the bottom,
stuck in an old vacuum-cleaner hose,
connected it to the exhaust-fan,
spray painted the whole thing
Allis-Chalmers orange,
draped some six-mil poly
down the front like an apron,
turned on the fan and

put the apparatus
over my head.

It clunked against my skull,
froze my ears and howled
like a jet engine.
I have to believe Dad found humor
in its creation and the indignity
of its crowning
upon my arrogant teenage head.

Religious Teachings

During seventh grade confirmation class
our minister described heaven
and the rewards of devotion:

"Imagine a corporate boardroom,
God sitting at the big desk
in the center,
around him desks are arranged
in crescents stretching to eternity.

God places the pious and devout
within sight of his desk.
The less ardent persist
in a sea of office furniture,
dispatching memos in paradise;
only those dappled by his radiance
would know what they missed."

I remember asking how,
if Cain and Abel
were the first-borne children
of the first people in creation,
how Cain could run off
and get married
after he axed his brother?

The pastor said
there were people on earth
not created in God's image.
This derailed the simplicity
of the whole creation deal,
so I figured
Adam and Eve
were the first Cro-Magnons,
and Cain must've run off
to live in lust
with a tribe of Neanderthals.

But before I was further instructed,
even before the city could
tear down Block E and
disperse prostitution
throughout the neighborhoods,
our pastor was arrested soliciting sex

from an undercover policewoman
on Hennepin Avenue.

He asserted it was a crusade of mercy,
all he wanted her to do
was get down on the floor
of his car
and pray with him.

Epiphany

Rainy morning in second grade,
recess cancelled.

Beneath fluorescent lights,
I hold a stack of mimeographed
barnyard scenes to be colored
in crayon with tedious precision.

Staring out the window,
rain washing down the panes,
lightning shattering into long,
broken crackles of thunder,
I experienced my first epiphany:
realized how much of my life
would be spent
filling in the shapes
drawn by others.

Sorties

When I turned sixteen
I got a job selling potatoes.

I had recently earned the
provisional driver's license,
and for a buck-sixty an hour,
joined a teenage fleet
trucking loads of
hundred pound gunnysacks
Into the inner-ring suburbs.

We set up on gravel lot vacant corners,
on the edges of crumbling strip malls,
next to Mexicans hawking
black-velvet tapestries of Elvis or
poker-playing bulldogs.

I leaned my spray painted plywood sign
against the tailgate,
topped a hundred pound sack with big russets
like I was told,
surrounding it with
smaller sacks of "dirty B's".

In the sharp winds of November I sold them
by the twenty-five, fifty, or hundred pounds.
I paced the frozen gravel,
making change and smoking cigarettes,
until the sun squinted through the powerlines,
and it was time to pack up my rattling field truck,
lumbering north on highway 10
toward an empty lot by the railroad tracks,
where we parked in shabby rows.

In the falling dusk,
old man Washburn stood waiting
as we emptied our pockets,
unloaded our unsold spuds,
and joined the growing huddle,
as more bald-tired stragglers
creaked across the potholes
In the blowing snow.

Grandpa's Living Will

Don't call an ambulance.

Grandma called at supper,
"Dad's had a stroke,
you better get up here."

We left our plates on the table
and got in the car,
twenty minutes later
we pulled into the dooryard.

Grandpa sat where he fell,
back against the sofa,
clenched a paper tissue
in the hand that still worked,
scrubbed at the carpet
where he'd pissed
his overalls.

On a farm what lives
dies in plain view,
by accident, harvest,
or slaughter.
Grandpa figured hospitals
for the slaughterhouse,
once inside,
you didn't come out.
Grandma only called the truck
for sick cattle.

Dad made the call,
had no compact
with grandpa
about hospitals.
It felt okay,
already too late.

I sat on the floor
beside him,
close like when I
was little.

He couldn't speak
but his eyes
were big,
crescents of white in the corners

like a steer's
pulled up the ramp.
I heard feet as Grandma opened the door,
scrambled out of the way.

Grandpa looked up
at the EMT's
then down,
wiped at the wet spot
with his tissue.

Hauled out through the kitchen
on a stretcher,
he grabbed the table leg.

He wasn't coming back,
but didn't wanna leave like this,
gone to market.

Seventeen

When I was seventeen
I helped Dad build a shed
for the tractor and pickup.

We cobbled it onto the side
of the corncrib,
built it from crap:
salvaged grey lumber,
un-peeled basswood posts,
creaky, rusted tin roofing that
banged in the wind.

A volunteer boxelder, rooted
against the foundation twisted itself
into a massive, spraddle-limbed beast.

I found it magnificent. Dad wanted it down.
It was a weed. It was in our way.

I was heartsick, argued to save it,
couldn't see killing a tree
for a rusty tractor and truck.

Dad relented.

We excised the shed's rear corner,
built around the trunk
and let it stand.

One year later it died.

Spike and the Rubber Vomit

Grandma had been up since 5 AM, putting together Easter dinner. It was noon, table set, serving dishes filled, guests arriving.

Uncle Fritz was Grandpa's brother. He wore loud ties and cool shirts, a junkman and practical joker who moved to the city and hung out with the Jewish tailors on West Broadway.

Uncle Fritz found his chair. Spike, Grandma's beloved German Shepherd, watched with intent. Fritz deftly plucked some gag-store rubber vomit from his pocket and flung it onto the seat of his chair.

Grandma set down a bowl of mashed potatoes. Fritz pointed to the vomit. Spike gazed up innocently.

The elements of a tragedy were in place: An invited guest dressed in his Sunday best, an unspeakable mess on his chair, and a shameless dog.

"Spikey!" Grandma spat, and slapped his snout. The dog yelped. Fritz snickered, snatched up the vomit, and sat down.

That was it.

Grandma never forgave herself for siding with Uncle Fritz and Fritz never acknowledged there was anything to apologize for.

Spike made out best; he licked every dish.

Easy Money

One Sunday at a kegger in the ballpark
by Diamond Lake,
Doug Swenson, recent high-school drop-out,
ass-crack squeezed above belt-less Levis',
bet five dollars
he could empty a plastic milk-jug of beer
in one gulp.

He tipped it up and it drained
down his throat
like dishwater.
Triumphant, empty jug hooked
from a forefinger,
he was paid off,
weaved around,
alone in his glory.

A few minutes later a jet of foam
arced from his mouth
like a fountain,
he suffered its velocity
awe-struck and powerless.

That afternoon,
as we played softball
in the shadows of tall blue silos,
he sat on a log,
head between his knees,
five dollars in his pocket.

Dad's First Psychedelic Experience

My parents were sleeping
in a pick-up camper
parked in the clearing
at Dad's hippy-cousin's homestead.

It rained for a week,
soil so saturated
the clay dissolved into
an oily paste,
mocha-colored puddles
lubricating goose and
goat shit
into greasy footing.

When the rain lifted to a drizzle
unleashing a prickly drone of mosquitoes,
we ran outside to play,

slid down the driveway
in our boots or on cardboard,
skidding down
that eroded
goose-shit slope
like some kind of
mudslide slalom.

Mom stayed in the camper drinking coffee,
reading books,
wishing she could go home.
She wasn't crazy about the Hippy Ethos,
didn't like livestock with cute names,
black bean chili in the dark,
or outhouses with picture windows.

That night I ended up in the kitchen,
among dropout homesteaders
and hangers-on
drawn from the bush like moths to fire.
Drinking beer and passing 'round homegrown,
Steve was hitting off the joint
when Dad pulled open the screen door,
walked in, sat down.

Dad was an unknown quantity.
People said he was the only guy

they knew who didn't *need*
to get high.

The room went silent,
circle moved Dad's way.
Steve shrugged
and handed him the joint.
It wasn't my hand, wasn't my decision.
Dad pinched it
off his finger,
took a drag,
passed it on.

The Universe exhaled,
lanterns smoked,
candles flamed,
people walked outside to pee.
Each time the joint came by
Dad took his hit,
poured himself another
cup of coffee.

Later, sky cleared, constellations
standing on their heads,
Dad climbed into the camper
and undressed.

I guess Mom busted him:
he was acting weird;
all he wanted to do
was curl up in the bunk,
boombox to his ear and
spin through the AM dial,
Lefty Frizzel,
and Paul Harvey,
fading into Little Rock.

My Mother's Stint as Outlaw

When I lived at home,
my friends and I would
smoke dope
on the back porch,
tap the ash
from our fried bowls
against the concrete
into Mom's hollyhocks.
Exotic plants
sprouted and grew
among the flowers.
We pruned and cultivated
them into the shrine
of our religion.

My mother
was enamored

with the handsome stranger
squatting in her flower bed.
When we told her
what it was
she couldn't believe
a plant so stately
could be as evil
as the government
made it out to be
and granted them asylum.

When I went away to college,
I taught Mom
pruning techniques
to maximize
the growth of flowers.
On weekends
she'd proudly exhibit
their maturity,
replacing
her empty nest
with these adopted children.

When the chill hit
in late September,
I came home,
pulled it out,

and hung it to dry
in a shed.
I was surprised
she didn't protest
outright cultivation for use,
but as a grower
harvest seemed natural,
and though declining a taste,
was gratified to hear
it was a superior product,
and even more,
that a Ziploc of buds
carried back to school
on Sunday nights
translated
into currency
at a high rate of exchange.
It was then
her farmer's soul
was activated.

It bought my groceries
and paid my rent,
a better cash crop
than soybeans,
so the next growing season
she tended the crop

without question,
wanted to do a part
in putting her boy
through college.
By mid-summer
crops were high,
weather was hot,
and the whole back porch stunk of skunk.
Though she disliked the odor
she knew its presence
signaled quality.

But all was not well,
the Reagan Years
slithered into our garden,
a policy known as
"Zero Tolerance"
was enacted and
disseminated through
the television.

My father was not happy
to learn that possession
of a plant
could mean the loss
of his house, car and property,
he urged its removal.

Greetings from Bullhead Country

But Mother was obstinate:
no one was going to tell her
what kind of shrubbery
she could have.

A state of paranoia
routinely observed
in growers,
grew in my mother
a condition recognized now
by Rainbow People
as "Green Energy."

The smell surrounding
the backdoor was
eye-watering,
though Mom insisted
it kept the flies down.

All was decided one sunny evening
in September.
Earlier that day,
before the three squad cars
catapulted up the driveway,
sirens wailing,
my father's ne'er do well cousin,
Frank the Tank turned up

in one of his sporadic,
unprovoked visits.

Mother never had much time
for Frankie's All-Star Wrestling wit,
generally left him
standing on the other side
of a screen door,
which is where
he made his discovery,
"You know what you've got
growing there don't you?"
"No." Mom lied.
"That's marijuana." Frank said.

"Well if it is, it's a very beautiful plant."
she replied.
Later as squad cars converged on the house,
lights flashing,
Mom, positive Frankie snitched,
walked out the door
to confess.
But the police were on a 911 call,
a man named Samborski
was having a heart attack,
she pointed to where he lived.

Shaken and reborn,
Mother tore out
the offending plants
and stuffed them deep
into the compost pile.

By the time I returned
to hear the news,
it had rained and
Mr. Samborski had died.

As I dug out
the plant's
moldy remnants,
I realized
this winter,
I would need to
get a job.

The Isanti Bounty Boondoggle

America was built on bounties, cash incentives paid out for the death of all beings declared varmint. Total war on the competition. To collect a bounty, one must deposit proof of destruction with the county clerk: a pair of feet, a tail, or a scalp.

When Grandma was young, she joined that crusade as a child mercenary. There were ten cent bounties on gophers, and on top of that, her father paid two cents a head for sparrows. She was a crack shot, owned a .22 rifle, but realized, if she paid fifteen cents for fifty shells, she lost a penny on every third sparrow.

Lawrence Welk bought his first accordion with the money he earned trapping gophers,
but Grandma was running a business. She reinvested a portion of her earnings on a dozen mousetraps and

set them on fenceposts baited with grain. When she caught enough sparrows to pay off the mousetraps, it was all profit.

On the pocket gopher front, she borrowed her father's "O" size leg traps and discovered a bureaucratic inconsistency that doubled her money. Their farm, located in Sherburne county, was a mile from the Isanti county line.

To prove on the bounty, Sherburne County collected front feet, Isanti collected tails.

An International Affair

During WWII my Mom and her brothers were playing in the woods on their farm south of Hanska. They found a uniform button with a swastika on it and ran home to show Grandma. They were sure there was a German spy hiding out there. Grandma shushed them and put it in a drawer and that was the end of it.

No one considered a more plausible explanation.

Across the nation, there was a manpower shortage. All able-bodied men were mobilized for the war effort, few between the ages of 18 and 40 remained.

Twelve miles away in New Ulm, a prisoner of war camp had been built for German soldiers. New Ulm was a German town, many P.O.W.s were happy to be removed from the war in a place people spoke their language.

The P.O.W.s were given the option to work for area farmers. They received fresh food and escaped the confines of the camp. Many had grown up farming back home and fell right into things.

Farmers' daughters faced their own manpower shortage and these young men were eager to fill the gap. Many returned after the war to settle down in rural Minnesota.

Less likely a spy or escaped prisoner hiding in the woods, more probable, Romeo and Juliet in the woodlot.

Lester

Standing around the kitchen table
at the farm,
everyone dressed to attend
Grandpa's funeral,
I turned to great-uncle Lester,
black suit coat over his
stripy bib overalls,
said
"See you at church."

"I'm not goin'," he said.
Stunned, I gasped, "Really?!"

"I don't like their music," he replied.

But Mom said later
it was cuz

he'd have to
take off his cap
inside.

He was tall and lean,
face like a hawk,
dark wounded eyes
below long bushy brows,
not much hair left on top.

Lester got pulled over
at the stop sign
down by Oris Sletta's.
He rolled down his window,
said "Whadja pull me over for?"

The sheriff pointed,
"You drove clear through that stop sign!"

"I know it," Lester told him,
"I never stop for that one!"

Lester avoided small talk,
yups, nopes, not much for goodbyes.
You'd look toward the end of the driveway
where he'd parked his Plymouth
and notice it was gone.

An established Norwegian bachelor farmer,
a youngest brother,
Lester never left home, never changed bedrooms,
farmed that one-sixty the rest of his life,
played cribbage at the cafe
watched TV by the stove,
at eighty-five, he clarified
with infamous brevity
why he never married:

"Too expensive."

At his own funeral,
attendance inescapable,
he was buttoned into suit and tie
with everyone watching.

No one thought to let him
wear his cap.

Scott Vetsch

Florence Told

How Ignatious caught his pinky
in the pumpjack and crushed it
nearly in two,

studied it a moment
before he opened his pocket knife,

snipped it off
like a green bean,

took one last look
and pitched it in the weeds.

How he snatched the crusty bandanna
from his pocket,

spit tobacco juice
on the stub,

wrapped it tight,
tied it,
and went back to work.

Grandpa's Birth Control

No toothbrush.
Boiled coffee.
Decades of Copenhagen.
A mouth not even a grandmother
could kiss.

Ruins

Decades of still-life pick-up trucks,
their shattered windows spilled across the seats
like crushed ice.

Tin cans scraped clean,
heaped together,
pitted and brown.

Flies buzzing in the afternoon sun.

A museum curated by time and weather,
on display
in an empty pasture,

beyond a barbed wire fence,

where the poplar woods
reaches down.

Don't let the tour guide fool you,
the great cathedrals of America

are piles of rusting junk.

New In-Laws

The Texan cornered Uncle Lester at the wedding,
bragged that it took him from sunrise to sunset
to drive across his farm.

"Yeah," Lester said, "I got a car like that too."

Who Took the "K" out of Fun-Pac

You know those little mini boxes of cereal,
the "Fun-size,"
part of a complimentary breakfast
at Motel 6?

You know how they come
shrink-wrapped together,
twelve at a time?

How it says "Fun-Pac" on the plastic wrap?

Wonder why there's no "K" in Fun-Pac?
Heard of industrial sabotage?

Dad worked in the photo department
at General Mills
in the Good Old Days,
when "Fun-Pack" still had a "K".

Before the Fun-Pack Ad Campaign
was launched,
Dad was sent out to
photograph the new product.

As "Fun-Pack" displays
were assembled in
supermarkets across America,
it was clear something
was wrong with the labels.

On the shrink-wrap
holding the boxes together,
where stencils that read "Fun-Pack" repeated across
each package,
the lettering had been cut in an odd way.

In a factory somewhere,
some guys, instead of cutting
the plastic between "Pack" and "Fun,"
cut it hundreds of thousands of times
between "Fun" and "Pack",
so instead of "Fun-Pack"
it simply read "Fuck".

Dad's Quest for Perpetual Motion

Dad believed the world could be powered by giant
drinking birds,
fields of them
rising and falling like oil derricks.

He kept dozens of the conventional size
bobbing on tables and countertops as an experiment
to see if they would eventually stop.

Mom *was* a perpetual motion machine;
washing dishes, sweeping floors, chopping onions,
browning hamburger.
The added motion of the bobbing birds
hitched to Dad's idleness
drove her crazy.

Watching TV, feet up in the recliner,
Dad conducted his research during commercial breaks.

Called out to Mom,
had she noticed any birds
slowing down?

Motherhood Before the Microwave

A dollop of ketchup and a hot dog
was the lunch I chose daily.

As the summer sun baked our
sandplain lawn brown,
children ran through the house,
screen-door slamming.

Mom was wearied by the repetition.
Worn down by demand.
Her days were like the wieners,
bobbing redundant
in boiling water.

By late July she sought release,
and in August came a revelation.

She dropped that first pale frank
headlong into her tallest plastic tumbler
and filled it with tap water
hot enough to draw the chill
from its skinless flanks,

then slid it onto a plate
to await my verdict.

It was pretty good.
I didn't even wait
for it to cool.

After the Storm

Two vultures spin like
black X's
in the tattered scud.

The sky is ragged;
red around the nostrils,
black around the eyes,
going through some changes.

A groundhog noses through
the alfalfa,
snapping down stems,

a dragonfly trembles
on a board
with cat-eye wings.

The sun reflects up
from the creek
in bright worming ripples
against the barkless bones
of a willow,
its grey bleached trunk
leaning across the pool.

A sprawling cottonwood
spills fluff
into the sky.

Elm branches
reach across
the water,

their twigs purpled
with buds,

more scattered
across the wet sand,

iridescent,

blown down
in the storm.

Tornado Alley

Out at Tony's people drink, stagger 'round a bonfire, jabber til the dew falls and nobody remembers the last sentence anyone said.

Theresa is Tony's law-school wife. She starts out cool and suburban, but at length spills her sorrow on your shoes. Her passion consumes water-glass whiskey-cokes like an Olds 88, burns childhood beatings to ash, chisels the memory of a five-month-home-delivery-miscarriage into a third-person narrative.

She wants to be sculpted to, painted to, desires music from the heart. "Sing to me Damnit!" and she don't care how good. Life gets alien on the great oak savannah, long cold tongues of prairie wedging between.

The baby brought them closer together, they buried it down by the willows somewhere.

Tony shoots a couple cats a week, but he can't get ahead; more claim the emptied fields. He traps coon too. The only way to keep 'em outta the corn. One night he butchered one and chunked it into a crock-pot with carrots, but it was so greasy and tasted so musky he switched over to beer.

Theresa spends each week white knuckling the highways and county roads. Traversing the prairie between one second tier city and the next: a semi-trailer lashed solitude coupling employment, home and school.

Home demands toil: firewood to cut, trim to paint, acorns to gather, rust to sand, sheds to build, lawn to mow. The struggle against decay is gargantuan, no time for thirst, only har-de-har-hars and crack a beer, arena-rock blasting out the windows at twilight.

Next morning she's tense and formal, she hardly knows you. The tap is either on or off, and if it don't get turned on soon, the whole thing'll rupture. That's Tony's job. He's the Quartermaster when he's not workin' overtime at the cabinet shop. It's whiskey and

Red Bull, 12-gauge shells and hydroponic weed. Tony mixes the drinks, grills the meat, rolls joints from tonight's paper-plate-pile of homegrown.

The weather bureau calls it a Tornado Alley. Land of the Straight-Line Wind. Straws are buried in the trunks of trees, metal stakes twisted like the gnarly black limbs above.

"C'mon." he says, "Grab a Red Bull and let's check-out the tree damage." Chainsaws yowl and whine. Tony and his dad went in together on a log-splitter, creating fuel from the destruction.

Choosing Darkness

In the summer
a two-horse Johnson
shunts my dreams
against life's
6 mile per hour
current.

Watching the water
I gain,
gauging the shoreline
I'm going nowhere.

But in winter,
my dreams,
preserved in cornmeal,
are baited
on a #8 hook

and dropped through holes
in the ice.

There's a whole universe down there,
and blindly I jig my grub toward
some cut-rate El Dorado,
 bouncing my sinkers
against its jewel-encrusted walls.

Bottom Feeder's Blues

Flat on my back,
across the floor of this rented room,
I stare out the window,
an exhausted meditation
on the night sky.
High above, the white belly
of a jet liner
passes over the city
like a shark
indifferent to the
singular existence of me
lost in a multitude
of lamp-lit windows
twinkling up from the depths.

Never before had I considered the plight
of the ignoble bottom feeder,

the scavenger fish;
assumed they swam
to the surface
like angels
when they tired of the ooze
on the ocean floor,
thickly tasting the shimmer of sun
with inarticulate lips.

My excuse to remain below,
smarmy and unimaginative,
is ironclad,
the song of a Newtonian swarm
arranged and sung in chorus:

I would leave the instant
air became water,
swim up to touch
that aeronautical pectus,
discontinue this roiling around,
flat-footed beneath gravity's law.

But the answer,
simple and practiced for generations
anchors me.

It's what I know.

Ice Fisher

He points across the ice,
there's Wayne, Chet,
and Trang.

In his dark house
observes fish
drifting across the gravel bar
like blown leaves,
sees panfish scatter
as a muskie
trolls beneath his hole
like a submarine,
so close
he could reach down
and caress
its slippery hide.

He's fished the city lakes
since he was a kid,
not a post-modernist,
he offers astute theories
on bait presentation
and a traditional
gathering of
goldenrod galls.

It's Sunday noon
and he's packing his sled,
has to go
eat dinner
with the wife.
Doesn't know what
they'll talk about.

She works full-time
in a nursing home,
has for years.
She only talks about
old people,
and he just can't stand it.

Delroy Calhoun Said

The one thing he learned from his dad was
if you gotta eat a frog
don't spend a lot of time lookin' at it.
If you gotta eat a lot of frogs
eat the big one first.

A Son's Inheritance

I'll carry your pain,
not reeling drunken
beneath its weight
or splashing
the overfull pail on the feet
of the unsuspecting.

Instead I will savor it
like the pit of some eaten fruit,
hold it against my tongue
in an unlit room.

Wait for the test pattern darkness
to hiss into dawn,
erase the memory of you,
playing your thumping, windy,
barrelhouse piano,

songs tromped out
to rally the troops.

A cherub's face cracking
upon its menopausal frame,
a mime's mask,
beneath which everything hidden fissures.

Where strapped-down longings
pushed through
like the roots of a windswept tree,
broke up the evenness of the lawn
that was supposed to make you happy.

Good Intentions

I bring my little girl
hooking trout on Stewart River,
drift an angleworm
down the pool
at Big Rock,
snag two
before they clam up.

Not like goldfish
carried home in a plastic bread bag,
gills agape,
hooks twisted out
and dead.

Behind her grandparents' house,
the transition from fish to fillet,
hacking through jewelry store skin,

subtle markings,
my jagged gashes.

She runs through the hawkweed,
while I dismember this beautiful creature
unattended,
make meat
from an angel.

I should have thanked it's spirit,
left a gift
for the surrender,
not forgotten it in Mom's refrigerator.

Next time I feel the compulsion to instruct,
we'll buy a can of pork and beans
and search together
for a can opener.

The Fisherman's Wife

It's not like Wayne's wallet
wasn't heavy enough
to hold his bait down in the current.

It's not like she's a bottom feeder or anything,
she's exactly the kind of fish
he wants to catch.

It's just that Wayne is Mr. Catch and Release:
he should've filed the barb off his hook,
but was daydreaming,
caught with his pants down,
she swallowed it and couldn't let go.

She's a fine piece of china,
leased by the paycheck,
trounced in bed with bored abandon,

hair spun with spray,
a dime-store halo of
Rumple-stilt-skinian gold,
her Barbie Doll pout crayoned
into a flash of genitalia.

Simultaneously across the sidewalks
of the world,
dogs are held virtual prisoners,
A canine Holocaust,
And what's the species thing
Got to do with pain and caging?
Chainsaws and fishhooks?
It's all slitting,
gaffing and cordwood,
all scalpels in a turbulent age.

The Weight

Mom smokes cigarettes on the deck,
winter and summer.
She's a great believer in the powers of tobacco,
would never quit,
says smoking makes life worth living,
cushions each hour.

Shoveling the deck after the blizzard,
I uncover coffee cans
overflowing soggy, brown butts
into the snow.

From the railing hangs a plastic tote bag
where she's dumped
the cans that came before.
The white sack sags brownly with
the weight of her habit.

Mom's an eat-off-the-floor
type of housekeeper,
a follow-behind-you-with-a-mop
kind of mom.
This doesn't follow.

I want to ask if I should toss it in the trash,
but realize it's no oversight:
she's building a monument.

With each cigarette,
she feels the immensity,
experiences the magnitude,
knows the exact weight
of what it takes
to live through each day
of her life.

Pissant Hill

On Pissant Hill
the verdict was clear:
live a good life,
attend church,
keep your allegiances in order.

Uncle George lived his
on the farm with sister Hazel
and her lapsed Catholic husband,
my grandpa Steve.

Walking west from town
south of Lake Fremont,
where County Road 4 skirts
the slough like a garter snake,
Uncle George pulled a nearly empty
pint whiskey bottle

from his coat pocket,
downed the last swallow,
tossed it in the ditch.

From his other pocket
he slid the one he just bought,
cracked the seal,
polished the bottle's lip with his
sleeve, took a slug.
Corked it and dropped it
back in his pocket.

It was a fine day.

The priest was paying another visit
to the farm, pleading
for grandpa's soul.
In the priest's eyes grandma Hazel
was nothing
but a whore.

Nobody called George's sister a whore,
leastwise not a priest. George told him
to pick up his undertaker's hat
and get the hell off their property.

The priest
didn't show much haste in leaving,
so George followed behind
punctuated his every step
with a kick in the ass.

Lost Currency

Grandma told a story about an old guy
she knew long ago, from another time.
I don't remember what she said about him,

just that she paused,
noting my confusion,
and poured us both a little more brandy.

Her summation is a fragment now,
an epigram in search of meaning.
She shrugged,

"He was a Belgian you know."

Frieda Sums it Up

Great Uncle Lester never married, I guess you could call Frieda the love of his life.

She lived in Essig; a German town on the prairie. Lester was from Lake Hanska; a two bar town, twelve miles south, where everyone came from Trondheim.

In it's day, that kind of kind of cultural miscegenation was a potent force. Brown-brick, beer and sauerkraut Catholicism was exciting if you were a Lutheran used to drinking watered down church basement coffee.

I never knew about Frieda, Lester came alone on holidays, never mentioned a lady friend.

Mom said back when she was a kid, Lester was a real looker. When he went out dancing it was quite a production. She remembered her grandmother heating up water on the cookstove for his Saturday night bath and Lester parting his black hair in the mirror over the kitchen sink.

I never knew him as anything but an owly old bachelor farmer in stripey overalls with a feed cap on his head and a black suit coat over that if somebody got baptized.

He never had running water, never took down that calendar from 1941, and died addled, at eighty-seven.

There weren't many people at the funeral, but when Frieda appeared in the back of the chapel, everyone turned to look.

The director announced the viewing was over and asked the mourners to find their seats. The organist was playing the first hymn, but Frieda was still in back, so my uncle took her by the arm.

"They're about to close the lid on Les," he told her, "Do you wanna have a last look?"

"No, " Frieda replied, shaking her head, "I had a good look."

It Used to Be All Woods Up There

Grandma said in the 1910's
a newlywed couple
lived up on the hill.

The bride was helping pull stumps
with the team
when a cable snapped,
caught her round the waist
and strung her guts
across the ground.

Grandma never told how many
days of grief the groom allowed
after the funeral
before he dragged himself out of bed,
hitched up the horses
and finished clearing
that field.

Carl and the Beanstalks

We were at Florence and Carl's for Sunday Dinner. As usual, the beans were baked, but this time bigger than navies; pink and mottled. Carl said he wasn't sure what kind of bean they were.

Carl and Florence found each other long after most people thought their chances were over. They lived together another forty years, until he died, a few months short of his hundredth birthday.

They were self-sustaining retirees, sharing a farmstead with her half-sister Norma. They supplemented their social security by gardening, canning, fishing, freezing, hunting, and cutting wood.

Their love of the world filled the windowsills with stones, pinecones and gnarls of wood, arrowheads, and bird nests. Carl told how a swarm of yellow jackets got ahold of him in the garden, how that infusion of cortisone cured his arthritis for a good long spell.

But what about the beans? He shot a Canada goose a few years back, he replied. Dressed it out and cut the crop open to see what it ate.

Inside he found 6 or 7 beans. Planted them outside when the sun came back. He collected what grew and planted again. In a few more years they had a row of beans to eat and reseed.

I know those beans now by name. I buy them at the store. But back in 1974, that was how the Pinto Bean came to Princeton Minnesota.

Best Corn I Ever Ate

"Hey Dad,
remember that time
we went fishing
and weren't catching any and
I said I was hungry,
so we ate the corn
we were using for bait?
This corn tastes
just like that."

The Intellectual

A pile of concrete rubble
was heaped twenty-five feet
from an empty dumpster.

A construction crew stood poised.

I, the boy who thought everything
could be solved by thinking,
sensed stalemate.

When the foreman asked;
"Who here knows how to use a shovel?"

I step forward,
the only one.

Proletarian Writing Workshop

When I was working
for Bruce Bacon,

doing carpentry jobs
on the farm,

he explained why he never completed
his thesis on Thorstein Veblen.

He told me every nail I drove
was another word
I wouldn't have to write.

Meditations on the Old Man

When Dad got tense you could tell,
he started clearing his throat.
You noticed a musky odor,
black hairs on his back
bristled through the weave
of his button-down shirt.

It was uncomfortable.

We cowered beneath a flattened tent
in the boundary waters,
electrical storm tearing up the night.
Mom and Dad's outstretched arms were backlit
     by lightning,
they braced the flapping fabric against the
     gale's surge.
Dad bucked us up,
"Remember kids, these are the good times."

Standing up to Dad was like
standing in a hurricane,
my sister saw what happened if
I did and hid under the bed.
She feared loud noises,
held her hands over her ears when anyone
pointed a camera her way,
expected a muzzle to extend from the lens
and fire.

Dad made his living as a photographer,
always taking pictures.

Dad looked like Jackie Gleason,
smoldered like Rod Steiger,
was funny like The Honeymooners.

Sundays at Grandma's we watched Disney
in the colors Tinkerbell splashed
across the screen,
but back home our black and white TV
was the light that lit.

Dad was a survival mechanism,
if you dropped him from a plane he'd bounce,
in a desert he'd live off his hump like a camel.

He was hard as a piglet, taut as canvas,
built like a barrel, sooty and greasy,
welding cap slathered across his scalp like
some infernal monk.

He was covered with black hair
like a boar or bear,
ate as long as there was food,
bulged like a bull snake.
The sun couldn't burn him,
he hardened up like a nut.
If he sat in a chair,
he'd sleep there good as a bed.
Grandma said when he was a kid,
if they ran into friends
on Saturday night,
he'd curl up on a newspaper
on the sidewalk and sleep.

Dad never inhabited the world of children,
his was a larval stage.

We used to dress up like him,
stuffing pillows into his old suits,
stamping up and down the hallway
in his black shoes,

giggling 'til Mom would say,
"I know what you're doing..."

One night after shooting a wedding,
too tired to carry his equipment
into the house,
Dad covered it with his suitcoat and
locked up.
Next morning he found a broken window:
camera equipment undisturbed,
suit-coat stolen.

The thief did not share his values.

A colleague from General Mills explained:
photographers nowadays
dressed like truck-drivers,
but in the '60's they were truck-drivers
trying to pass as photographers.

Dad photoshopped the eyes out of family photos and
switched them around.

Dad trained us to be ready
for any deployment,
for any disaster, by land or by sea.
Our camping trips were

rehearsals for refugees,
our belongings piled high upon
Dad's home-designed, hand-built, catamaran,
our two-horse Johnson
wide-open against the
Mississippi's six-mile per hour current.
With a bicycle lashed on top,
we were truly all-terrain,
our yowling Siamese cat tethered to a thwart
by a length of chain.

Dad taught us
that like our cat,
straining to reach a distant shore,
we'd best learn to love what we had,
and like that cat we huddled
in our life jackets,
accepting what fate handed us.

Dad was too cheap
to buy a truckload of soil
to backfill the footings
around the new garage.
We waited for pocket-gophers
to mound up dirt each night
as they tunneled beneath our yard,
then skimmed it off with a shovel.

We simply adjusted our expectations
to their scale of production.

Dad fashioned sunglasses
from a pair of empty negatives.
He stared directly into the sun
during a solar eclipse,
and burned a hole in his retina.

We were a family that
rooted for the underdog,
drank Pepsi-Cola, drove Chevies.
Santa left off-brand Lincoln Logs and
fake M&M's
beneath a Scotch Pine.

Dad's ode to the Mechanical Age was a homestyle
pipe-organ powered by steam, a merry-go-round
lacking ponies and joy. Dad fed the fiery hole shovels
of coal, holding a musical thought. Cheeks smudged
with grime, he tuned each organ pipe with a wrench,
tightened hissy plumbing, dressed squealing belts,
oiled squeaky pulleys, squeezed grease into every
zerk: The conductor of a truly infernal music. Sitting
on kitchen chairs, we endured Sunday afternoon
concerts behind the garage, sipping Kool-Aid as Dad
midwifed the music of his heart into open air.

He was a romantic, an idealist, considered himself an optimist; mystified that dire predictions were viewed as pessimism. It wasn't sound business: it was a crusade, buying back everything he couldn't afford, laminating his dreams together from scrap-wood and discarded machinery. Process not production.

"Build it plumb and level," the old carpenter advised, "It's the answer to every question. If you build outa square, you gotta calculate how far it deviates and add that to each step. After a few steps the calculations become complex."

That's how Dad lived his life; he reinvented gravity, then reconfigured the rest, recalculated every pebble and leaf.

Anything less than perfection held no interest, neither did production. It was all about perfection, and once it was nailed, he was done. If no one saw the difference, he knew and that's what mattered.

Dad stopped feeding the birds to cut down his odds of contracting Avian Flu.

He wouldn't travel, viewed the world with the eyes of Laurel and Hardy, Popeye and Scheherazade.

Sunday nights driving home from Grandma's, I dozed in the backseat. As we left the highway, I could pinpoint our location by the rhythm of Dad's driving: accelerate, shift, brake, a quick turn, the whine of the transmission beneath my head, and I knew a beat before, when he'd depress the clutch, like music: the melody of the road home.

After taking a tool sharpening class together, I imagined his childhood schoolhouse behavior: he was disruptive, meant well, was vaguely charming, but kept walking around the classroom, talking to people, diverting their attention. The teacher tried to get Dad to do his work, looked again and he was across the room telling stories, even classmates wanted to find him a project. He needed attention, he couldn't be fenced, he was my dad.

Grandpa told him: when you're shocking grain, face what you've done, not what you haven't.

When I was a kid I liked lakes, they're placid, easy to fish, easy to boat in. Lakes bored Dad, he dragged the family down creeks and rivers; water that moved. Rivers and creeks were murky, they carried sediment and stank. The current made bobber fishing impossible. I was forced to cast. I learned to watch eddies and swirls, respect undertows, submerged rocks, rapids, spillways, and falls, to watch for snags and deadheads. I learned to imagine what lay beneath those turbid waters.

We discovered swamped boats and canoes stolen by spring floods, caught weird, exotic fish, learned to see the river's floor by observing the swirls on the surface. Best of all it came from somewhere and was going somewhere else, like AM radio waves at night, and if I chose to, I could go with it.

Big fish are found in areas that suit their needs. Reading water is a study of finding the best places. Fish live in ten percent of the water. I grew up never expecting the best. We lived on stunted, sandy soil. My dream of a lake home was a shack by a swamp.

I never joined the competition for great things. I couldn't recognize them, they were alien. I could appreciate beauty, but never chased it. I'd been socialized to see what I could attain, then stepped aside for the alpha-dogs. The best was invisible. If I noticed a beautiful woman, immediately I looked around her for the damaged one. If I was fishing a stream, I gravitated toward marginal water, where the smaller fish congregated. It was all I could see.

It's what I saw instead of good water. I justified it as unrecognized, which was true periodically, when I pulled the rabbit out of a hat. But mostly I watched other guys haul big fish out of flawless water and flogged the rest, extracting oil from shale and all the energy it entails.

That was my niche, my shtick, pulling off another miracle, seeking my ten percent within the bounds of the remaining ninety. I strived for the flash, for the wow, to be a magician, hard-scrabble farmer bogged down in the sand. I had to be better. Dad didn't do it to be mean, he just readied me for the water he knew I'd be fishing, the water he'd fished his entire life, the only water he knew.

About the Author

Scott Vetsch, author of *Tilt-A-Whirl*, (Calumet Press, 2025) lives and works as a carpenter in Minneapolis, Minnesota, remodeling historic homes. He graduated from the University of Minnesota with a bachelor's degree in English Literature and remains an avid reader. He is also a participant and supporter of the literary community, and a founding member of the Bosso Poetry Company, which has been performing Spoken-Word, music and poetry in and around the Twin Cities since the late twentieth century. Ecology is his religion. He still lives by the same river he grew up on--the mighty Mississippi--fishes it when he can and crosses it daily.